KT-493-548

Renewals
01159 293388
www.library.bromley.gov.uk

Bromley

THE LONDON BOROUGH
www.bromley.gov.uk

Please return/renew this item
by the last date shown.
Books may also be renewed by
phone and Internet.

Comparing Past and Present

Going to School

Rebecca Rissman

Raintree is an imprint of Capstone Global Library Limited, a company incorporated in England and Wales having its registered office at 7 Pilgrim Street, London, EC4V 6LB – Registered company number: 6695582

www.raintreepublishers.co.uk
myorders@raintreepublishers.co.uk

Text © Capstone Global Library Limited 2014
First published in hardback in 2014
The moral rights of the proprietor have been asserted.

Edited by Rebecca Rissman, Daniel Nunn, and Catherine Veitch
Designed by Philippa Jenkins
Picture research by Elizabeth Alexander
Production by Helen McCreath
Originated by Capstone Global Library Ltd
Printed and bound in China

ISBN 978 1 4062 7147 8
17 16 15 14 13
10 9 8 7 6 5 4 3 2 1

British Library Cataloguing in Publication Data
A full catalogue record for this book is available from the British Library.

Acknowledgements
We would like to thank the following for permission to reproduce photographs: Alamy pp. 7 (© redsnapper), 10 (© ClassicStock); Corbis p. 9 (© Yi Lu/Viewstock); Getty Images pp. 6 (Keystone-France/Gamma-Keystone), 11 (Siri Stafford/Lifesize), 12 (Brooke/Topical Press Agency/Hulton Archive), 13 (Christopher Futcher/the Agency Collection), 14 (Kurt Hutton/Picture Post), 18 (Kurt Hutton/Picture Post), 23 (Kurt Hutton/Picture Post); 20 (Mary Evans Picture Library); Shutterstock pp. 5 (© Monkey Business Images), 15 (© AVAVA), 17 (© Pressmaster), 19 (© Zurijeta), 21 (© Monkey Business Images), 23 (© AVAVA); Superstock pp. 4 (Underwood Photo Archives), 8 (Underwood Photo Archives), 16 (ClassicStock.com), 22 (ClassicStock.com).

Front cover photographs of pupils and teachers of the Steamer Class in the Washington School, Massachusetts reproduced with permission of Library of Congress (Lewis Wickes Hine), and a primary school pupil doing an assignment reproduced with permission of Getty Images (PhotoAlto/Odilon Dimier). Back cover photograph of primary school pupils reading books in front of a blackboard, 1930s, reproduced with permission of Superstock (ClassicStock.com).

We would like to thank Nancy Harris and Diana Bentley for their invaluable help in the preparation of this book.

Every effort has been made to contact copyright holders of material reproduced in this book. Any omissions will be rectified in subsequent printings if notice is given to the publisher.

Contents

Comparing the past and present

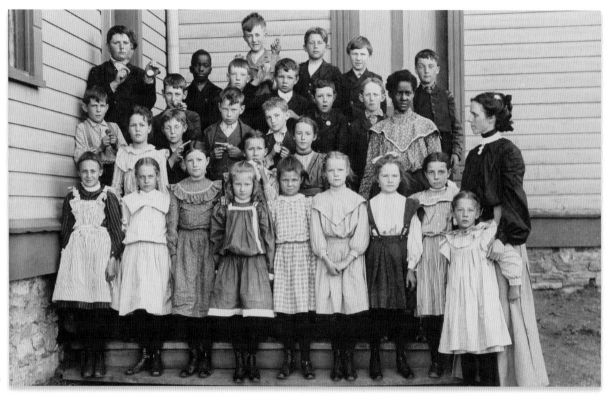

Things in the past have already happened.

Things in the present are happening now.

Schools have changed over time.

Schools in the present are very different to schools in the past.

Schools

In the past most schools were small. Some had only one room!

Today, many schools are very large.

Getting to school

In the past many children walked a long way to school.

Today, many children ride
in cars or buses to school.

Classes

In the past children of all ages were in the same class.

Today, most schools place children
into different classes by their ages. 13

School supplies

In the past many children wrote on small blackboards.

Today, children write on paper or
type on computers.

In the past schools had few
books for children to read.

Today, school libraries have
many books for children to read.

In the past children learned things by asking teachers

and reading books.

Today, children can use a computer to learn things. They can also ask teachers and read books.

Lucky pupils

In the past only some lucky children could go to school.

Today, many children can go
to school.

Then and now

In the past children enjoyed going to school. Today, children still enjoy school!

Picture glossary

 **blackboard** dark writing surface. People write with chalk on blackboards.

 **computer** machine that helps people write and learn

Index

Notes for parents and teachers

Before reading

Talk to children about the differences between the past and present. Explain that things that have already happened are in the past. Ask children to describe their activities from the previous day. Tell children that all of those activities happened in the past. Then explain that the conversation you are having now is happening in the present.

After reading

- Explain to children that the experience of going to school has changed in many ways over time. Ask children to describe their classroom, emphasizing the school materials, class size, and technology. Then ask children to brainstorm about how their experience is different from what children might have experienced in the past.

- Ask children to turn to pages 14–15. Show children the two images, contrasting the technology in modern classrooms with what children used in the past. Then ask children if they can think of any other technology they use at school that did not exist in the past. Keep a record of their ideas on the board, and add any that they might have missed. Remember to include electricity, telephones, and running water.